How Indian Immigrants Made America Home

COMING TO AMERICA
THE HISTORY OF IMMIGRATION TO THE UNITED STATES

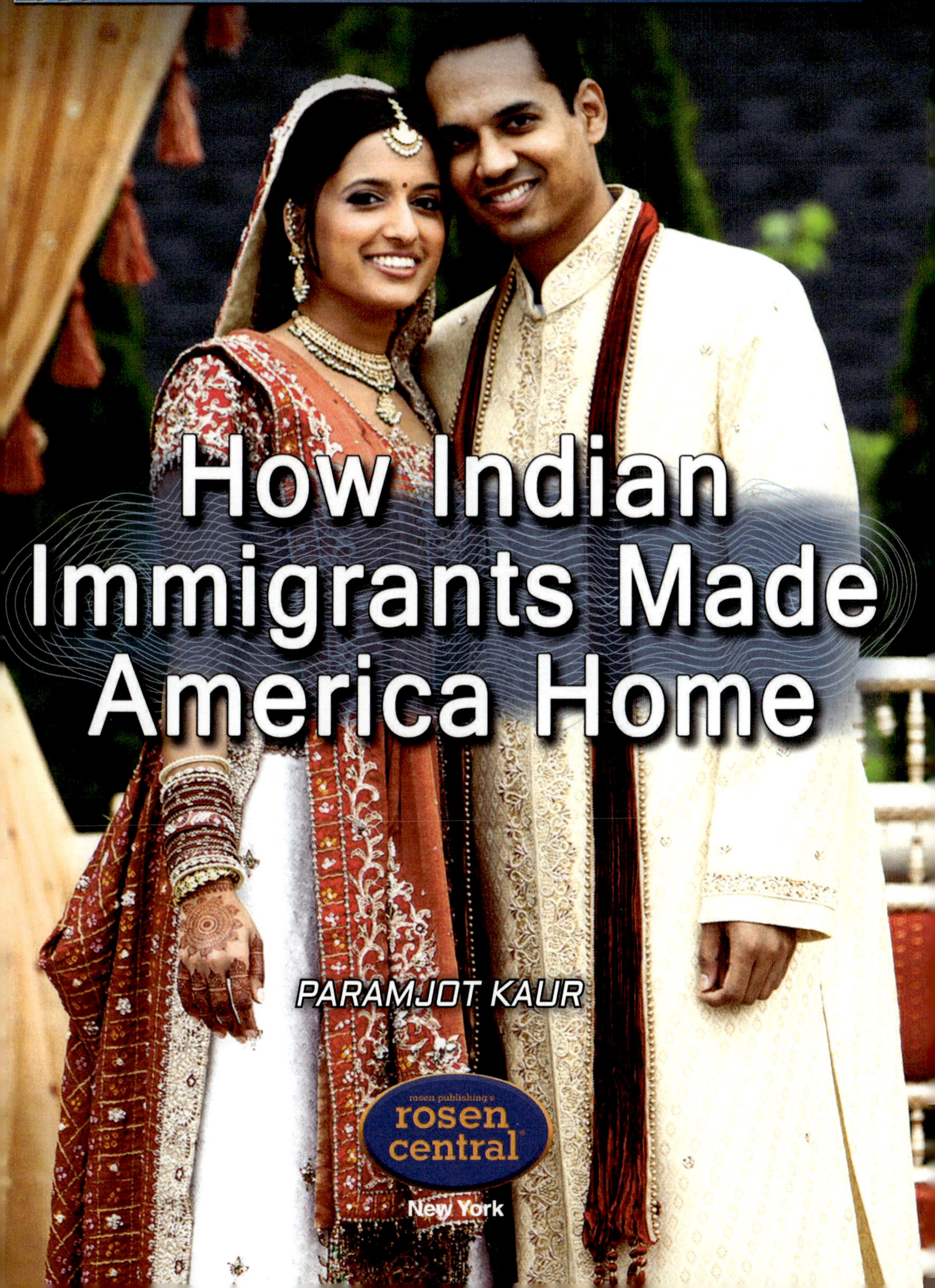

How Indian Immigrants Made America Home

PARAMJOT KAUR

rosen publishing's
rosen central
New York

To my parents, Karm Singh and Rajwant Kaur, and my family

Published in 2019 by The Rosen Publishing Group, Inc.
29 East 21st Street, New York, NY 10010

First Edition

Library of Congress Cataloging-in-Publication Data

Names: Kaur, Paramjot, author.
Title: How Indian Immigrants made America home / Paramjot Kaur.
Description: New York : Rosen Central, 2019 | Series: Coming to America: the history of immigration to the United States | Includes bibliographical references and index. | Audience: Grades 5–8.
Identifiers: LCCN 2017044348 | ISBN 9781508181231 (library bound) | ISBN 9781508181248 (pbk.)
Subjects: LCSH: East Indian Americans—History—Juvenile literature. | Immigrants—United States—History—Juvenile literature. | India—Emigration and immigration—History—Juvenile literature. | United States—Emigration and immigration—History—Juvenile literature.
Classification: LCC E184.E2 K38 2019 | DDC 305.89/1411073—dc23
LC record available at https://lccn.loc.gov/2017044348

Manufactured in the United States of America

On the cover: An Indian couple is dressed for a traditional wedding ceremony.

CONTENTS

Introduction

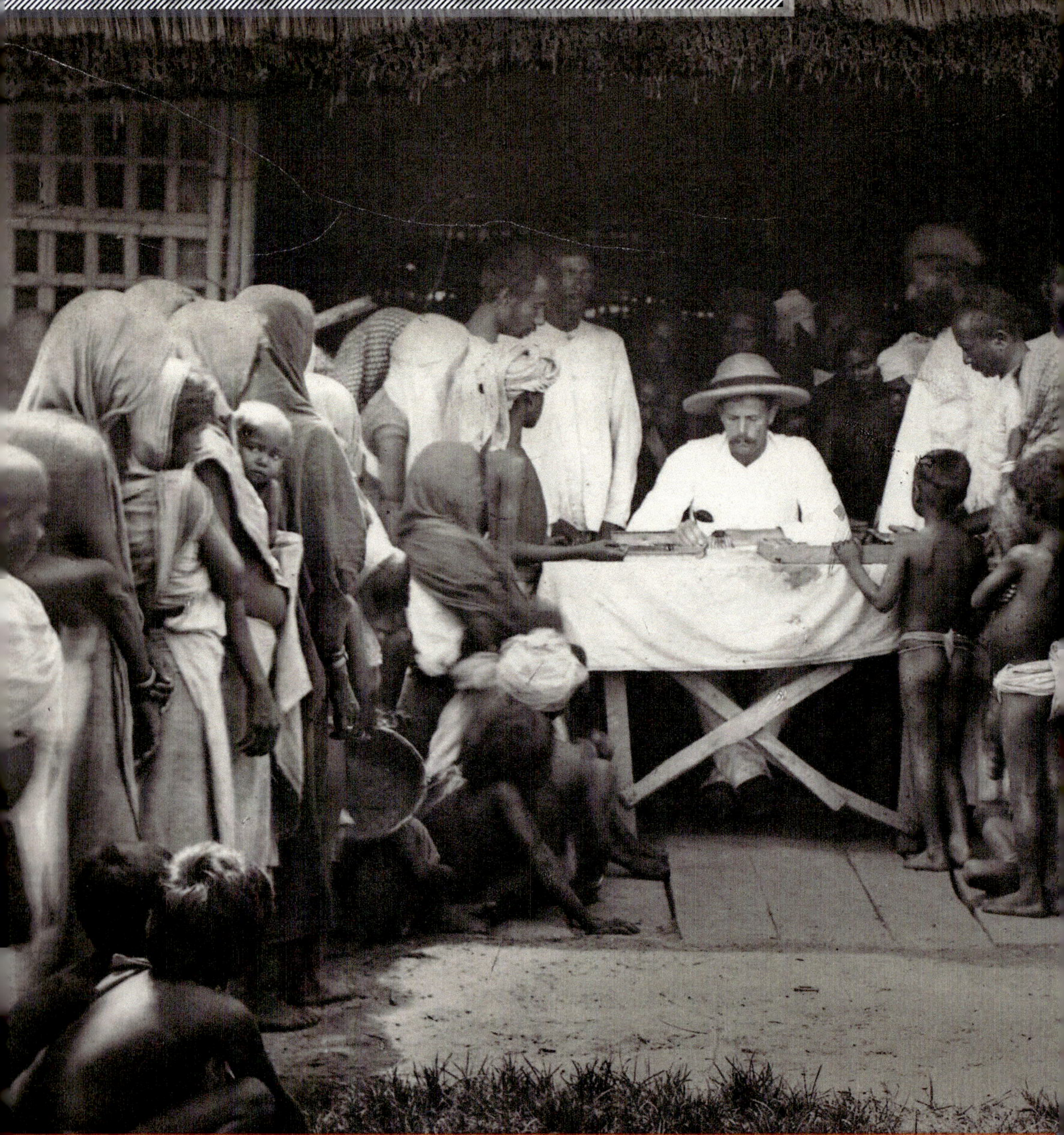

A European employer is filing and distributing payments to Indian laborers in the tea industry, which expanded due to demand for Indian chai. Laborers included children and elderly people.

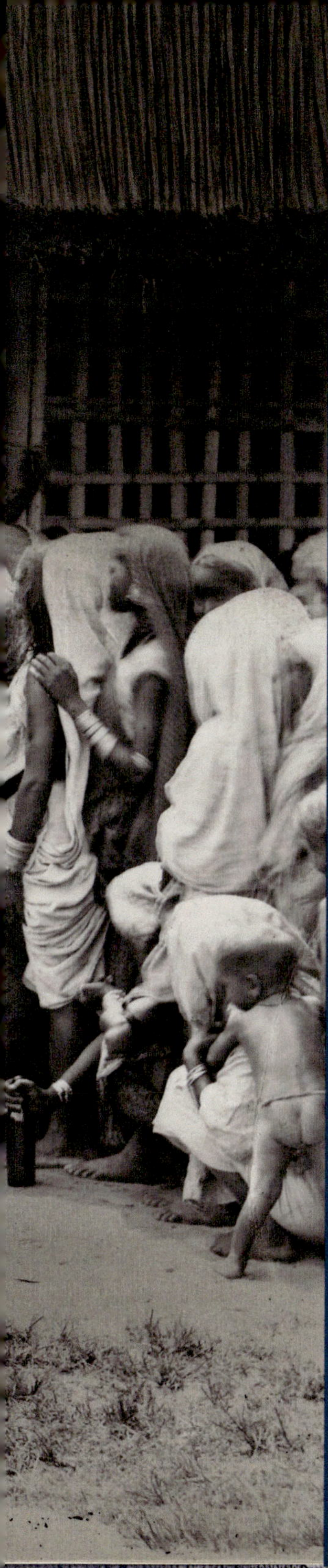

The act of traveling from one nation to another may appear to be simple. But what it looks like changes according to the details of individual situations. For the Indian diaspora, the picture of immigration throughout the decades shifted along with the struggles, cultural changes, fear, hope, and, success.

Indian immigration can be divided into three major waves. The first wave was in the early 1900s. In that era, rural farmers, weary from the oppressions of living in British India, arrived in California. At this time, immigrants took on the task of adapting to circumstances. The second wave of immigration in the 1960s offered hope. Travelers were eager to find a better life in America. And finally, the third wave, of the 1990s, brought highly skilled workers. Immigration was now a tool for success. America, with its changing culture and economy, had become the nation of immigrants.

The origin of the diaspora is the Republic of India, the home to nearly 1.3 billion people. People there speak twenty-two major languages, including Hindi, English, Tamil, Telugu, and

Marathi. These languages have traveled to the United States as well, through the tongues of the 3.5 million Indian Americans. The religious variety of the diaspora is also rich. Hinduism, Sikhism, Islam, Jainism, and Buddhism are some of the many practiced religions of Indian Americans. Temples, mosques, and other religious centers dot the Indian map and have also been established in the United States. Although India is only one-third the size of the United States, it's the world's second most populous country; China is the most populous country.

Developments in Indian history led to the dispersal of the Indian diaspora. When the British Raj was established in 1858, India became a colony of Great Britain. India gained its independence in 1947. Shortly after, India was divided into two sovereign states: India, the Hindu state, and Pakistan, the Muslim state. This is referred to as the partition. Hindu-Muslim clashes escalated. Bursts of violence resulted in unsafe living conditions. And India's weakened economy after World War II struggled to support the millions of refugees of the partition.

Indian emigrants who came to the United States shouldered the burden of the turmoil in their homeland and the burden of being victimized by the racism and xenophobia that became regular experiences. Prosperity was a goal that remained elusive to many as the protection of the law didn't extend to them equally in practice. But survival and perseverance have preserved those Indian immigrant communities who remain today.

CHAPTER ONE

Early Immigration in Times of Trouble

One of the earliest factors driving Indian immigration was the British occupation of India. The British had arrived in India as traders in the 1600s, and over time they established deep political roots that culminated in the colonization of the entire country. Discrimination was rampant under the British Raj, but such problems did not reside only in colonial India. Early immigrants found themselves in a foreign land among people who rejected them because of their brown skin, clothing, and accented speech.

TENSIONS BOIL OVER DURING THE BRITISH RAJ

India was known as a jewel country because of its exotic spices, silks, teas, and cotton. Its flourishing economy in the 1800s attracted international traders, the most influential of which included the British East India Company, which arrived at the port of Surat, Gujarat, in 1608. The company took advantage of the weakening Mughal Empire after the death of Emperor Aurangzeb in 1707 and quickly worked to expand beyond Bengal, its first acquired state, in 1757. By April 2, 1849, the company had annexed the state of Punjab.

Following the British East India Company's rise to power was the Indian Mutiny of 1857. During the mutiny, Indian sepoys turned on the British officials in Bengal and Delhi. They were resisting forced westernization, the replacement of the Indian aristocracy with British officials, the annexation of states, and the wave of Christian missionaries trying to convert Hindu citizens. A bloody first war for freedom had begun.

Rumors that Enfield cartridges, components of the rifles used by the British army, contained cow and pig grease further angered Hindu and Muslim sepoys since the cow is considered to be holy to Hindus. Similarly, the pig is an impure animal to Muslims.

When the rebellion failed to remove the British, the British government decided to directly rule over India. This period

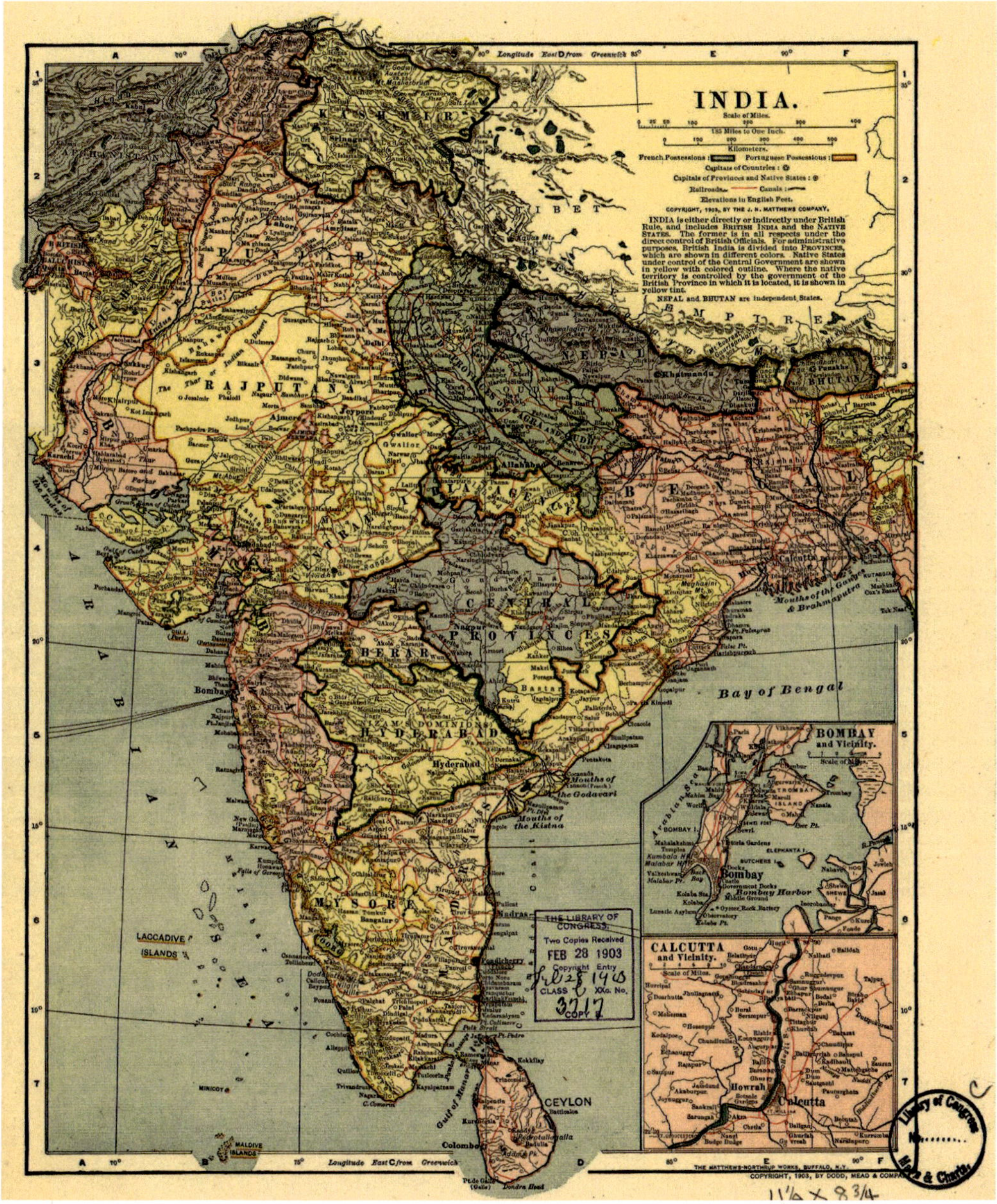

This 1903 map shows India under British rule, before the partition. Territories include modern-day Bangladesh and Pakistan.

is called the British Raj. Britain ended the British East India Company and the Mughal Empire by jailing Mughal emperor Mirza Abu Zafar Sirajuddin Muhammad Bahadur Shah Zafar, testing the tolerance of Indians across the country.

THE BRITISH RAJ

The British presence in India lasted 190 years. The British Raj, in particular, was established in 1858. During the British presence, India experienced a harsh tax system and other forms of revenue collection that severely weakened India's economy.

In 1877, Queen Victoria was proclaimed the empress of India. That title was meant to convey that India was under the direct rule of the British government.

During the British Raj, millions of Indians joined Britain's armed services and fought for the British in both world wars. On the societal front, officials held the aim of reversing India's supposedly backward culture. They sent Christian missionaries to conduct religious conversion and educators and scholars to teach British history, and they forced the Indians to use the English language.

THE FIRST MAJOR GROUP OF INDIAN IMMIGRANTS

The state of Punjab had an abundance of cash crops, so officials adopted a paternalistic attitude toward it because of its economic value. However, the control those officials imposed ignored the needs of those who lived there. Peasant farmers faced distress because of land theft. Corrupt zamindars, or landlords, ran the financial credit system. Farmers who relied on this system quickly found themselves in debt and then in debt foreclosure. Revenue-collecting officials demanded a set contribution, even during times of poor harvest. These zamindars decreased the possibilities of financial success through land ownership for farmers. Thus, the new system of fines created to modernize Punjab, including land regulations regarding inheritance and residence, established a modern feudal system.

This oppressive environment pushed agriculturalists from the state of Punjab to become the first major group of Indian immigrants to travel to the United States in the early 1900s. Some of them had also served in the British Indian police and armed forces. Tired of the disadvantages of living under British India, the men donned their traditional turbans, or head cloths, but traded their kurta pajamas, or long shirts and pants usually made of cotton, for Western clothes like suits and button-down shirts.

They soon found that white Americans harassed Indian people in the United States on a regular basis. Jane Singh, a research specialist at the University of California, Berkeley, whose Punjabi father immigrated in 1906, commented in an *LA Times* article, "You never knew if you went into town if someone was going to hassle you." Indian men removed their turbans and cut their hair. They hoped that changing their appearance further would help to avoid the hatred that their cultural signifiers unwittingly attracted. Having to navigate outright racism and evaluate their loyalty to their culture left Indian immigrants struggling to answer the question of how they should fit in.

THE FIRST NATURALIZED INDIAN IMMIGRANT

Akhay Kumar Mozumdar had traveled to the United States in 1903 as a lecturer and writer to become a part of the New Thought movement that began in the United States during the nineteenth century. Mozumdar left Calcutta, West Bengal, (modern-day Kolkata) in 1903 for Seattle, Illinois, to become a spiritual teacher. He faced difficult language and cultural barriers, but by 1906, he was speaking fluently in English and was even called a "Hindu brother" in the *Theosophical Quarterly Magazine* because of his ability to connect and relate with other members of the New Thought movement.

In the years 1912 to 1913, Mozumdar took on the Naturalization Act of 1790 and the Naturalization Act of 1870 that declared US citizenship to be granted only to "free white persons" and "persons of African descent," respectively. Mozumdar argued that he was a member of the high-caste

A. K. MOZUMDAR

OF LOS ANGELES, CALIFORNIA

under the auspices of the

School of Psychology and Divine Science

during the SUMMER INSTITUTE, June 10 to 21

ONE GROVELAND TERRACE

Well Known People Speak With Enthusiasm of Mr. Mozumdar and His Course in "Master Wisdom"

Mr. Mozumdar has resided in this country during the past thirty-two years, confining his activitie to the Pacific Coast until some years ago, when he was first called to New York City, where his fam as a philosopher and author of The Life and the Way had preceded him. Since then, he has visited th larger cities of this country lecturing and teaching.

His book, The Conquering Man, published some years ago, has reached a circulation of over fift thousand, and that without one particle of advertising except that given by enthusiastic readers. A number of copies found their way into Columbia University. When he was in New York he addresse the student body of the Theological Department of that institution.

"Of all the teachers, and we have had many, to whom our church doors are open, no one has been more acceptable than Mr. Mozumdar. I count on the judgment of my men more than I would my own. Many of them are professors in Columbia, Union, etc.; they are unanimous in their approval. Whenever Mr. Mozumdar desires to come to our church, our doors will be flung wide open for him.

—DR. E. H. EMMETT, Pastor of Manhattan Congregational Church of New York City.

"Of all the Courses in 'Practical Christianity' I have attended with various fine teachers, the Lessons by Mr. Mozumdar on Master Wisdom have been the most practical, complete and convincing. The study of Body, Molecular, Electric and Divine Vibrations and the Cosmic Ray has been a revelation, and has lifted me out of untold depths.

—MRS. F. H. SHEPARD, Shepard Schools of Music, New York City.

"Mozumdar's course plunged me at once into a laboratory method of doing things with expedition and power. I had expected theory, I got practice; I looked for philosophy, I got operative science. I had shopped around with courses of instruction before. They all seemed like kindergarten work; Prince Mozumdar's like a postgraduate course. I cannot thank him enough for the push his lessons give me toward action and reality away from bookish theories."

—JOHN SEAMAN GARNS, School of Psychology and Divine Science, Minneapolis.

"I do not know of any spiritual teacher that I consider so clos to the spirit of the Christ as Mr. Mozumdar. He has that perfec transparency that is a combination of what they say are the out standing qualities of Ghandi, humility and confidence; humility i the outer and perfect confidence in the inner. I feel that any on who perfectly comprehends his writings and puts them into expres sion in his life will possess the secret of the ages."

—GLENN CLARK, Macalester College, St. Pau

"How I appreciated your wonderful class! It was indeed wonderfu that you could simplify (by the aid of your illustrations) your in structions and make them so easily understood. You eliminated th non-essentials and presented the Truth in such a clean-cut, commor sense manner, and without sacrificing the beauty and spiritual sig nificance of your Message."

—GEORGETTE BANTA, President Chicago Psychology Club

"Never have I heard so clear, so logical and so beautiful a exposition of the real gospel of Jesus the Christ as that of Princ Mozumdar. He is indeed a Messenger of God. His inspired teach ing is in the highest degree simple, helpful and practical. Beyon a doubt he illumines the way to God-Realization."

—DR. ANNE VON HELMHOLTZ-PHELAN Late Professor of English Literature, poet

Mr. Mozumdar will give a course of ten lessons in "Master Wisdom" at the Summer Institute June 10 to 21, conducted at the School of Psychology and Divine Science, One Groveland Terrace

Mozumdar's teachings on the New Thought movement were celebrated in America. His literature and lectures were circulated among academics at institutions such as Columbia University.

Hindus of India, a pure and exclusive group that connects to the Aryans, the Indo-European invaders of northern India in 1500 BCE. The Aryans were (and still are) considered to have been a subdivision of the Caucasian race. Mozumdar's argument satisfied the naturalization laws according to United States District Court for the Eastern District of Washington judge Frank. H. Rudkin. Rudkin gave the green light for Mozumdar to be naturalized in 1913.

Mozumdar's citizenship aroused many questions, especially the question of how much whiteness was needed to satisfy the naturalization law.

CULTURAL AND RELIGIOUS PRESENCE

According to Jasbir Singh Kang's writing in "Punjabi Migration to United States: A Story of Great Tenacity," by 1910, approximately six thousand men had arrived in California. They were mainly laborers who found blue-collar jobs in California and neighboring states in the agricultural, lumber, and railroad industries. The growth of this community led to the founding of the first Indian religious center in the United States in 1912: a Sikh gurdwara in Stockton, California. The agriculturalists embraced areas like Southern California's Imperial Valley, which held cotton and lettuce fields. The Imperial Valley, among other immigrant regions, was also rich in the growth of new cultures, such as the budding Mexican-Hindu culture.

The Sikh Gurdwara Sahib of Stockton, California, was founded by a Sikh immigrant committee. The committee was mainly composed of men who belonged to the first wave of laboring immigrants.

Indian women faced more difficulties than men when going through immigration screening in the early 1900s. As a result, most male laborers who arrived in the United States were unmarried. Many ended up marrying Mexican women, who often worked as cotton pickers in fields that were leased to Indian immigrant men. According to research done by the

University of California, the first marriage between a Mexican and Indian was between the years of 1916 and 1917 in the Imperial Valley.

The intermarriages produced a mixed community that was called by various names, including Mexican-Hindus, Punjabi Mexicans, Mexidus, and half and halves. Although there were men who were Muslim and Sikh, many non-Indian people assumed that Indian immigrants were Hindus until the 1990s. Unlike many historical instances of exogamy, in the mixed marriage community of the Imperial Valley, the men in each marriage were Indian, and the women were Mexican.

EARLY PERCEPTIONS OF INTERRACIAL MARRIAGE

The general population viewed interracial marriage as foreign and shocking in the early 1900s. Discrimination against interracial couples was frequent because there was an ongoing effort to curb the mixture of races. Some thought that the American culture and ideals would become diluted if natives married foreigners. Similarly, for Indians, marrying outside of one's culture or religion was taboo. In some areas of India, the taboo remains. This did not stop the marriage between Indian immigrant men and women of other races.

The Mexican-Hindu community did not last. Apart from societal prejudice, there were religious and cultural conflicts in the community. The men followed their faiths of Hinduism, Islam, and Sikhism, and the women followed Catholicism. The languages English, Spanish, Hindi, Punjabi, and Urdu coexisted. As the children grew up, they found themselves caught between cultures. Indian fathers abhorred Western practices like dating. Mexican mothers, who were often much younger than their husbands, were in favor of Western culture and practices. The community experienced high divorce rates, and the children grew up with their mothers, where they were expected to speak English and Spanish and practice Catholicism.

UNFAVORABLE REACTIONS TO IMMIGRATION

Hardworking immigrant laborers found jobs by agreeing to be paid less to do more work in lumber mills, agricultural industries, and railroad companies. This was the labor situation for Indians in California.

Many in the labor community did not celebrate the newcomers. On May 14, 1905, several labor unions created the Asiatic Exclusion League (AEL) in California to oppose the immigration of foreigners who sought job opportunities that white workers were likely to pursue. According to proceedings from the AEL's first annual convention that were published in 1911, the organization was founded on the suspicion that Asian immigrants were "utterly unfit and incapable of discharging the duties of American citizenship" and "a degrading and contaminating influence to the best phases of American life." The word "suspicion" is appropriate because members of the league were intent on assuming that their prejudices were correct—they made no effort to investigate the truth of their claims.

Efforts by the AEL to keep immigrants from working in lumberyards and mills were successful. Those efforts caused migrations from California to Bellingham, Washington. But some in Bellingham weren't pleased at the new Indian presence. On September 4, 1907, the AEL decided to continue their work of terrorizing the displaced Indians. A mob of four hundred to five hundred men attacked Indians in their homes in an incident that came to be called the Bellingham riots. They beat the Indians and robbed them, and the police arrested four hundred of them afterward. Six Indians were hospitalized as a result of the episode.

On the following day, the Indian community fled Bellingham. This incident was remembered one hundred years later, in 2007, when Mayor Tim Douglas issued a public acknowledgment of the events and called September 4 a "Day of Healing and Reconciliation," according to a joint proclamation of the City of Bellingham and Whatcom County, Washington.

Indians would face another conflict concerning land ownership in 1913, when the California Alien Land Law prevented the ownership of land by "aliens ineligible for citizenship." To adapt, Mexican-Hindu fathers put their land in their American children's name (when they had American

The "Mexican-Hindu" communities that grew in the 1910s included Valentina Alvarez and Rullia Singh, who are seen in their wedding picture.

children). Others formed secret partnerships with white landowners to legally own the land but share the profits. This sharing was a gamble that sometimes led to treachery.

On the international front, British forces were keeping tabs on the growing Indian American community. Newspapers like *Free Hindustan* and the *Hindustanee* were founded to advocate for Indian freedom. Indian American students banded together to create political groups like the Ghadar Party to oppose the British occupation of India. The Ghadar Party was a radical group that wanted to overthrow the British Raj by conspiring with the German government. William Charles Hopkinson, an Anglo-Indian British official who placed surveillance on Indian "radicals," infiltrated the group and exposed their plot to the British Indian government for violating a neutrality treaty between the United States and Great Britain in regards to British India. British and AEL efforts continued to limit immigration.

By 1917, the Immigration Regional Restriction Act of 1917, also known as the Asiatic Barred Zone Act, ended immigration from most Asian countries, including India.

CHAPTER TWO

Clash of Interests, Skin Tones, and Laws

With new immigration laws created to diminish immigration from Asian countries, people wondered what would happen to the immigrants who had already come to the United States. Immigrant scholars did not face as many restrictions to entry, but they still had to survive and try to make a life in the United States. Various answers would emerge between 1917 and 1946.

THE US LAW SYSTEM CHANGES THE RULES

The United States Immigration and Naturalization Services (INS) followed the 1790 and 1870 laws that extended citizenship only to "free white persons" and "people of African descent." Some Indian immigrants were naturalized because they shared features with southern Europeans. The question of whether Indians could legally be naturalized was overlooked until it was brought up in the case of *United States v. Bhagat Singh Thind*.

Bhagat Singh Thind arrived from Amritsar, India, and became a University of California, Berkeley, graduate and World War I veteran. Unlike many other immigrants, Thind kept his turban and beard. His three years of citizenship were brought to a halt in 1923 due to the joint decision of US Justice George Sutherland and Chief Justice William Taft. Both officials agreed that Indians could not assimilate into the American culture as easily as European immigrants, in spite of Thind's success.

The case of *United States v. Bhagat Singh Thind* affected the citizenship of previously naturalized Indian immigrants, including a man named Vaishno Das Bagai.

Vaishno Das Bagai moved to San Francisco in 1915. Bagai, an educated and wealthy man, found happiness when he was naturalized in 1921. He proudly ran a store called Bagai's Bazaar. He was so confident in his circumstances that he had given up his British passport and voluntarily lost his legal standing in that country.

Then, the 1923 decision *of United States v. Bhagat Singh Thind* revoked his citizenship. The California Alien Land Law forced him to sell his store once he was categorized as a noncitizen, thus disconnecting him from his means of survival and his proudest achievement. And then, he was denied the reissue of a passport that would allow him to return to his homeland.

Bagai committed suicide in 1928. He wrote the following in his suicide letter and addressed it to the *San Francisco Examiner*: "I do not choose to live the life of an interned person; yes, I am in a free country and can move about where and when I wish inside the country. Is life worth living in a gilded cage? Obstacles this way, blockades that way, and the bridges burnt behind."

FURTHER RESTRICTIONS ON THE AMERICAN DREAM

Because of the general desire of lawmakers to preserve an image of the American identity through keeping a homogeneous population, a new act was introduced to further restrict immigration. The Immigration Act of 1924, also known as the Asian Exclusion Act, created an origins-quota system. The law stated that the number of immigrants allowed to enter the United States from any foreign country was equal to 2 percent of the residents of that country already residing in the United States. The law relied on data from the 1890 US census as its reference. Asians were excluded from this law, so Indians

The Asian Exclusion Act, passed in 1924, ran counter to the ideals expressed by Emma Lazarus in her poem "The New Colossus," shown here on a plaque inside the Statue of Liberty, which it describes.

seeking refuge from oppression in British India could not rely on American support. The total number of Indian residents was 2,500, according to the census.

The oppression Indians faced under the British Raj was what set the stage for Indian admiration for the United States, in reality a hardly better alternative. The United States had held enchanting stories of tall buildings, fancy cars, and well-paying jobs. When the concept of the American Dream was introduced to the public in 1931 in *Epic of America,* a book by historian James Truslow Adams, all dreams and hopes of a better life were channeled into it. Adams's book described it as a promise for a land of opportunity and a rich quality of life.

A significant detail from his book was the potential for success for women. He wrote that it was "a dream of social order in which each man and each woman shall be able to attain to the fullest stature of which they are innately capable, and be recognized by others for what they are, regardless of the fortuitous circumstances of birth or position." This passage gave hope for gender equality, a caste-free society, and the ladder of success for all groups of people.

Reality seemed to bear some truth to this possibility in the San Francisco Bay Area. Technological successes like the new aerospace industry, the newly founded Ames Research Center, and the creation of the first transistor indicated that America was the place to be if one desired to contribute to furthering these new advances. Even if white Americans and American institutions were hostile, it wasn't a given that Indians couldn't be a part of those advances.

STAGNANT HOPE

Twenty-three years after *United States v. Bhagat Singh Thind*, US law concerning immigration and naturalization rights of Indians remained the same. World War II was beneficial to the US economy since it ended the Great Depression. It was also beneficial for US immigration because it ushered in the opportunity for Indian immigrants to push for change.

After World War II and at the start of the Cold War, the United States emerged as the capitalist leader of international

Mahatma Mohandas Karamchand Gandhi advocated for Indian independence from the British Raj through nonviolent measures in India. He is often seen as a symbol of India's freedom.

affairs. This leadership role implied future communication with Asian countries, including India. J. J Singh, president of the India League of America, predicted that this would occur and used that prediction to gather legal support for India's independence. The Indian market still held the potential for producing textiles, gold, and agricultural products, but only Britain reaped the benefits. Singh pitched Indian independence and the value of trading with a free India to the US Congress. The first step would be supporting Indians, both residents and immigrants, through the Luce-Celler Act of 1946.

SILVER LININGS IN 1946

Immigration rights were not discussion topics that were confined to immigrant communities. When the Luce-Celler Act was passed, which allowed one hundred Indians and one hundred Filipinos to immigrate to the United States each year, scholars and writers like Albert Einstein, Upton Sinclair, and W. E. B. Du Bois supported it. Albert Einstein commented that the new act was a progressive stance toward peace and prosperity. Historians and activists also justified the act by bringing forth stories of several Indian immigrant men who served as soldiers in the American army, including Bhagat Singh Thind and an earlier soldier, Raghunath Banawalkar, who served in France from 1918 to 1919.

President Harry Truman signed the act on July 2, 1946. It granted naturalization, voting, and property rights to Indians. An annual quota of one hundred immigrants was set. For the first time, Indian immigrants could apply for citizenship while embracing their cultural and religious background instead of trying to represent themselves as being a member of another race.

CHAPTER THREE

Freedom Across International Borders

The twenty years following the signing of the first act that enabled Indian immigration, in 1946, were ones of victory. India prevailed over the two-hundred-year-old British occupation—a sigh of relief that was felt across global borders. Educated Indians in the United States began to rise to leadership positions, and the Los Angeles Philharmonic Orchestra in 1962 performed under the principal conductorship of Zubin Mehta. The flag of integration and a hopeful future was waving. Indians in the United States did not feel so forlorn anymore.

INDIA GAINS INDEPENDENCE

On August 15, 1947, the fruit of resistance movements that had been in place since 1857 bloomed when India gained its independence from Britain. The final success came through a movement called Quit India that civil rights leader Mahatma Gandhi led, which relied on a philosophy of nonviolence. When World War II ended in 1945, Britain was weakened and gave way to agreements to leave India. Troops began to leave in 1947.

The Indian victory came at a cost. The partition, the division of the country into India and Pakistan, occurred

On August 15, 1947, the flag of newly created Pakistan was presented by a Pakistani group of advocates at the Lancaster House in London.

soon after. The division came to be seen as necessary because Britain encouraged religious conflicts as a means of cementing its control, but those conflicts didn't disappear when British power no longer reigned over that territory. Violence in Pakistan continued in a civil war that led to the creation of Bangladesh. An estimated one million people were killed as fifteen million people rushed to the country that favored their religious identity. India's economy was crippled.

BRITISH VS. INDIAN INTERESTS

The British pushed for the United States to deport Indians who formed pro-independence groups in the United States. The British also tried to prevent Indians from leaving India for the United States. Naturally, Indians didn't care for the British attempting to exert influence over them in those ways.

When the British Raj ended, Indians long held back by harsh taxes and low wages slowly regained their financial footing. Daniel Houston Buchanan mentions an example of the extreme income inequality that existed between the British and the Indians during the British Raj in *The Development of Capitalist Enterprise in India*. Indian workers at Tata steelworks received an average annual salary of 240 rupees, whereas British staff and officials received an average annual salary of 13,527 rupees.

The Luce-Celler Act enabled Indians to go to the United States during this era. But the United States wasn't the only available choice for them. Ironically, many Indians who fled the violence that ensued after independence immigrated to the United Kingdom to take advantage of the high demand for unskilled labor that Britain needed to recover from the war.

THE FIRST INDIAN IMMIGRANT POLITICIAN

Some educated immigrants had the goal of attaining higher education and then returning to India. Among this group was Dalip Singh Saund, the son of wealthy contractors from Amritsar, Punjab. Saund immigrated to the United States in 1920 and studied agriculture and manufacturing at the University of California, Berkeley.

After graduating from college, Saund moved to the Imperial Valley to become a lettuce farmer. It was there that he first encountered the reality of the Alien Land Law of 1913, specifically the fact that immigrants weren't allowed to own land. He began to study law independently and soon joined lobbyist efforts to advocate for Indian independence and naturalization rights. He also worked to support his new family, consisting of his Czech American wife, Marian, and young son, Dalip Singh Jr. On December 16, 1949, he was naturalized and soon after registered to vote as a Democrat. By 1952, Saund had risen to the position of a judge in Imperial County, California. It was around this time, in 1950, that Mozumdar reapplied for the

Congressman Dalip Singh Saund joined the US House of Representatives in 1957. He was the first Indian elected into American government. Saund was inspired by Abraham Lincoln and Mohandas Gandhi.

citizenship that was stripped from him as a result of *United States v. Thind* and was naturalized under the reformed laws.

Saund was a firm believer in Indian and American ideals, and he was a follower of Mohandas Gandhi and Abraham Lincoln. When he ran for Congress in 1956, the Indian community supported him. He even managed to get an endorsement from John F. Kennedy, then a US senator, who said:

> Judge D. S. Saund has proved conclusively his understanding of and devotion to the basic

Congressman Saund (*far left*) poses at a Congressional Coffee Hour group with President John F. Kennedy (*center*).

> meaning of our American ideals. After reading the moving story of his tireless and patient struggle to attain full citizenship rights for his countrymen and for himself, you will understand a measure of the love he bears for his America and for her people. We need this man's wisdom and loyalty in the Congress of the United States. The election of Judge D. S. Saund will promote international goodwill and greatly advance the cause of world peace.

In 1956, Dalip Singh Saund was elected to the US House of Representatives from California's Twenty-Ninth Congressional District. He was the first Indian man to make a place for himself as a leader in American government, succeeding in a difficult feat that was celebrated around the world. He served two full terms and was in his third when he suffered from a stroke. Saund passed away in 1973. His portrait was displayed at the Capitol to commemorate his service to the US government.

CIVIL RIGHTS ERA USHERS IN CHANGES

During the 1960s, civil rights activists questioned laws based on racial bias, especially the Immigration Act of 1924's 2 percent national-origins-based quota system for all foreigners. The origins system had constricted mass migration and led to families living apart for years. For Indian immigrants, there

President Lyndon B. Johnson signs the Hart-Celler Act, which removed the origins quota system. The act was signed on Ellis Island in New York City.

was no room for flexibility as the quota remained at a strict one hundred persons per year.

Representative Emanuel Celler of New York and Senator Philip Hart of Michigan proposed the Immigration and Nationality Act of 1965, also known as the Hart-Celler Act. It introduced the removal of the origins quota and supported higher rates of immigration. The postwar era had begun; and the United States had the responsibility to uphold its international leadership and progressive attitude for accepting people of all races and backgrounds. The act capped immigration at 170,000 visas from the Eastern Hemisphere, with no single country allowed more than 20,000 visas. Immediate family members were exempt from the rule. During the ceremony in which President Lyndon B. Johnson signed the Hart-Celler Act into law on October 3, 1965, on Ellis Island, he said, "From this day forth, those wishing to emigrate into America shall be admitted on the basis of their skills and their close relationship to those already here." Immigrants now had naturalization, voting, and property rights.

UNITED STATES OF AMERICA

CHAPTER FOUR

The Post-1965 Immigration Boom

The new era of immigration laws was one of thriving communities and large diasporas. There would even be new ways for families to join their settled loved ones. But nativist Americans saw Indian immigrant advancement as a threat, and the political environment in India devolved into one that left Sikhs, in particular, afraid for their safety.

ACCELERATED IMMIGRATION

Between 1952 and 1965, records from the Immigration and Naturalization Services (INS) indicated that family immigration cases were granted 86 percent of visas that were requested. This meant immigration was pretty open for wives and fiancées. The new wave included married men and large families. This demographic makeup is in contrast to the first wave's mainly male unmarried laborers. By the 1960s, 27,189 immigrants had arrived.

Between 1980 and 1990, the US census of 1990 reported the number of immigrants had grown from 31,858 to 57,992. California, New Jersey, Texas, New York, and Illinois became very diverse states that housed the thousands of arriving families.

The demand was high for skilled labor. There was a shortage of military physicians in the United States as service member physicians declined to re-enroll in the military when their tours of duty ended. According to a 1977 article in the *Washington Post* called "Military Has Severe Doctor Shortage," those doctors knew they could earn more money as civilians. Technology giants like IBM and the aerospace industry were hoping to draw scientists and engineers to work for them. And Indian scholars were working in the political sphere. Among them was Joy Cherian, who became the first Indian American commissioner of the United States Equal Employment Opportunity Commission in 1987. A year later, Har Gobind Khorana, an immigrant, received the 1968 Nobel Prize for Physiology.

Nobel Prize–winning Dr. Har Gobind Khorana, then working at the University of Wisconsin, stands at a chalkboard during a meeting.

WORKING INDIAN WOMEN IN SOCIETY

Unmarried, highly skilled people were also arriving from India. For the first time, large numbers of women were traveling to the United States. With the American Dream supporting the success of both men and women, working women took their chances with their careers and lives in the Indian diaspora. By 1980, the Asian American Women in America Organization, the first collective gathering of Indian immigrant women, was founded.

Going to the United States was not only a chance to start a successful career—it was also a battleground for social and cultural changes. These changes included gender roles. Through interviews that Ramya Vijaya and Bidisha Biswas, authors of *The Indian Immigrant Women and Work: The American Experience*, conducted, they found that many Indian immigrant women also appreciated emigrating from India to avoid arranged marriages and restrictions to social freedoms. Working women defied the stereotype of the traditional Indian housewife, who typically stayed at home. As independent people, they weren't as invested in the idea of arranged marriages and chose their suitors through dating and meeting new people.

THE H-4 VISA

The H-1B is a visa that gives workers the right to work in the United States. The H-4 visa is an extension of the H-1B visa because it allows the spouse and children of H-1B visa holders to come to the United States. It could work like this: A foreign man who held an H-1B visa would get hired in the United States and then get married. If his wife were a foreign national, then she would then be eligible

(continued on the next page)

(continued from the previous page)

Angirekula Sreekanth poses with his and his relatives' US visas at a Hindu temple. Thousands of devotees of all faiths hope to have their prayers answered by receiving US visas allowing them to live and work there.

for the H-4 visa, and it would allow her to enter the United States.

According to *Women in the World*, around 90 percent of H-4 visa holders in the United States are women. Around 80 percent of H1-B visa holders are South Asians, specifically Indian and Chinese men and women who work in professional fields like information technology (IT) and engineering.

(continued from the previous page)

The path of working women was very different from that of wives of H-1B visa holders. A spouse who holds an H-4 visa would likely not experience the United States the same way that an independent working woman who entered the country did. She would only have been exposed to Indian norms concerning the matchmaking process and expectations of domestic life.

The visa itself mandated some debilitating social effects. Wives of Indian workers were not allowed to work under the H-4 visa. Many of these women suffered from depression, loneliness, and frustration. However, a recent law change in 2015 qualifies H-4 visa holders to apply for a work permit called the Employment Authorization Document.

CULTURAL TENSIONS

A xenophobic backlash met this Indian wave of immigration into the United States. In 1987, New Jersey Indian residents found themselves experiencing so-called anti-Hindu attacks by a white supremacist gang called the Dotbusters. The name was meant to mock the traditional bindi, a red dot worn by Indian women between their eyebrows. The gang ignorantly assumed that all South Asians were Hindus. The fact that similar events dated back to the early 1900s proved that the ignorance of xenophobic actors hadn't been addressed.

Resentment toward corporations hiring foreign labor took on a dangerous form. On September 27, 1987, a group of teenagers attacked a thirty-year-old Indian man named Navroze Mody. He was so badly injured that he fell into a coma. Four days later, he died.

The mayor of Jersey City, New Jersey, Anthony R. Cucci said the attacks were "an animalistic approach to territorial domain." There was a misconception that immigrants were replacing Americans, despite it being commonly recognized that American educational institutions weren't incentivizing education in science, technology, and engineering to the extent necessary for those industries to have the workers they needed.

POLITICAL TURMOIL IN INDIA

Tensions between ethnic groups were not foreign to India in 1984. The Indian government's discrimination against Sikh Punjabis, including the overlooking of Sikhism as a religion, had been going on for a while since India achieved its independence. In the 1980s, political and religious leader Jarnail Singh Bhindranwale began gathering a massive group of Sikhs to oppose and resist. A march he led in 1982 resulted in the police inflicting violence upon the marchers. Thousands of activists were killed, and more than thirty thousand were arrested. When Bhindranwale pushed for militant action as the means of resistance, Prime Minister Indira Gandhi responded

THE CULTURAL "DOT"

Many South Asian women—followers of Hinduism and Jainism—traditionally wear the bindi, a simple red circle on the forehead. "Bindi" translates to *bindu* in Sanskrit, and it relates to the third eye. The third eye represents a person's connection to higher consciousness. The bindi has also become a fashion item worn in Indian celebrations, such as weddings or the festival of Diwali, also known as the Festival of Lights. Diwali is the Hindu celebration of good over evil.

Sometimes, Americans or people of European descent who aren't Hindu or Jain wear the bindi. Usually, they do it as a fashion statement in a setting like a music festival. However, wearing the bindi as a means of following (or setting) a trend is highly offensive to the Indian community. Participating in an aspect of another culture just to look cool disrespects what that culture stands for. This type of participation is called cultural appropriation, or repurposing part of a culture to gain cool points or to make a profit.

with Operation Blue Star. The operation was a military invasion of the Golden Temple in June 1984, one of the holiest places of Sikhism, to arrest Bhindranwale. Bhindranwale was shot to death. There were also 83 civilians killed, and 249 other people were injured.

On October 31, 1984, two of Gandhi's Sikh bodyguards, Beant Singh and Satwant Singh, assassinated her. The result was the 1984 genocide of 2,800 to 8,000 Sikhs. Immigration became a matter of safety, and the number of Sikhs leaving the country surged before 1984 ended. Refugees fled to the United Kingdom, Canada, and the United States.

IMMIGRATION IN THE 1990s

President George H. W. Bush signed a reformed version of 1965's Immigration Act on November 29, 1990. The revision increased the number of permanent work visas, especially for highly attractive skilled labor. This was a positive change for the growing population of engineering professionals in India.

The act was divided into five categories with varying priority. The first category was

Indira Priyadarshini Gandhi is shown in the 1970s, a decade before her assassination in 1984. She was India's third prime minister and the first woman to lead the country.

"priority workers," highly skilled professional workers with "extraordinary ability," such as scholars and top company executives. The second contained "advanced professionals and those of exceptional ability," such as PhD holders. The third category was for skilled labor, and the fourth was for religious workers. The last category was for business investors. The law also created a lottery system to award random visas for immigrants. Incoming immigrants who weren't a part of a settled immigrant's family were usually a part of the first three categories.

The mixture of skilled and unskilled labor made for communal development. Neighborhoods that came to be called Little India developed in Chicago, San Francisco, and New York City. These were bustling neighborhoods of shops and cultural centers. They held grocery stores containing Indian foods, music and movie stores selling Bollywood and Tollywood movies, jewelry and clothing shops, and restaurants that served Indian cuisine. Other store owners sold idols of deities in religious shops.

These Indian communities helped strengthen the presence of Indian culture. For other ethnic groups, the shops drew in curious shoppers and sparked a love of Indian cuisine.

CHAPTER FIVE

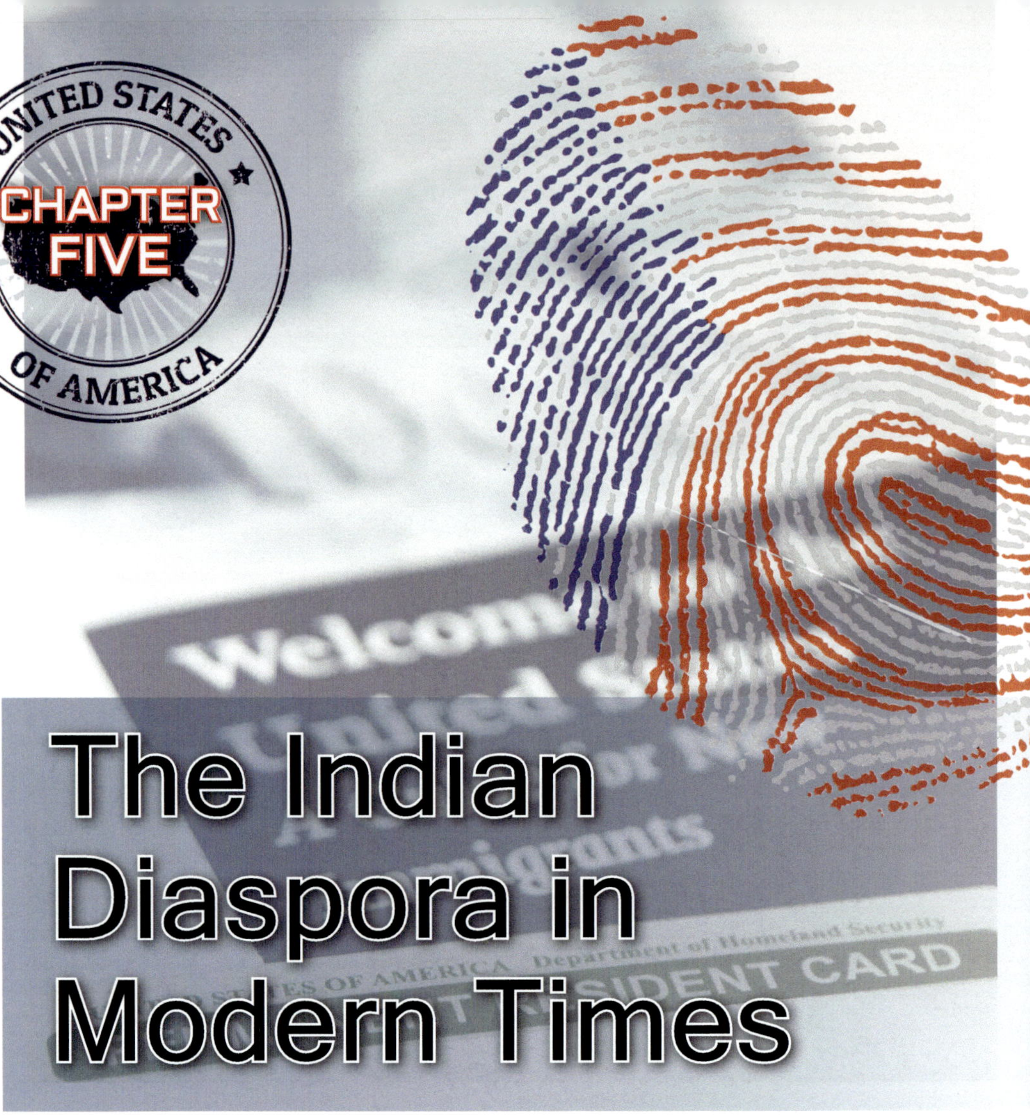

The Indian Diaspora in Modern Times

The children and families of the third wave of Indian immigration reflect on the way their relatives raised the flag of Indian communities in what had been a nation devoid of South Asians. Silicon Valley has become a sphere of great success for Indian IT workers, engineers, and scientists. Indian politicians have risen in the US government, working in departments similar to their predecessors of the 1960s. The creative worlds celebrate the vibrance of Indian entertainers, who continue to bridge the gap between Indian and American culture. However, the struggle to battle xenophobia toward the ethnic Indian community has not ended.

THE TECHNOLOGY GENERATION

When India expanded its economy in 1991 and gave greater autonomy to the private sector, the technology industry began to grow rapidly. The south Indian state of Bangalore gained acclaim by hosting technology giants like Amazon in 2013 and producing nearly thirty thousand engineering graduates every year, earning the title "the Silicon State." According to a research article by the Columbia School of Business, one of every three visas is received by an Indian in the technology sector, especially from the state of Hyderabad. The successful wave of technology professionals was the perfect fit for America's Silicon Valley.

The rise of the technology generation was beneficial to the American economy. Vinod Khosla, an Indian immigrant, cofounded the Silicon Valley–based corporation Sun Microsystems. Sundar Pichai was named the CEO of the international giant Google in 2015. Similarly, Adobe and Microsoft CEOs are also Indian Americans, Shantanu Narayen and Satya Nadella, respectively. These companies employ thousands of workers, both American born and immigrants.

Sundar Pichai, named Google CEO in 2015, sits with a group of female technology leaders in India. Pichai immigrated to America in 1993 to study at Stanford University.

Scholars Devesh Kapur, Sanjay Chakravorty, and Nirivankar Singh, coauthors of *The Other One Percent*, called Indian immigration "a major asset" to the United States. However, Indian immigration has revealed some telling trends.

When it comes to Indian immigration, the receivers of American visas are not entirely random. Scholars, students, unskilled and skilled laborers, and families each come from specific circumstances. Kapur, Chakravorty, and Singh explained in their book that the socioeconomic and educational circumstances of third-wave immigrants have a significant impact on whether immigration is possible at all. Wealthy families have the funds and connections to attain quality education. Expensive private institutions likely offer a quality education, including small classes that teachers conduct in English. Therefore, it is likely that a student who travels to the United States or another country for higher education or to work is fairly wealthy.

IMMIGRATION FUEL

Every year, thousands of Indians leave India to find a higher quality of life. Professionals like doctors, engineers, lawyers, and business executives enjoy high wages in the United States. Those high wages earned by Indian Americans make up the highest median household income of all ethnic groups. The US Census Bureau reported a median income of Indian American households of $103,821 in 2015. The fact that the US dollar holds more value in comparison to the Indian rupee is also a contributing factor to the appeal of the United States. Financial freedom and job successes inspire others to join the Indian diaspora.

INDIAN, INDIAN AMERICAN, OR AMERICAN?

The question of identity has been in flux ever since the earliest Indian immigrants set foot on US soil—in fact, it still is. Assimilation has always been an option, but that could mean giving up one's culture entirely.

The racist laws of the 1900s that settled cases based on skin tone and ethnicity and the xenophobic attacks of the 1980s furthered identity struggles. Was it better to not identify as Indian to gain an advantage, as A. K Mozumdar had done in 1913?

Indian values include preserving the family unit, utmost respect for elders, and supporting parents once children have successful careers. Older, more conservative generations found the West to be odd. Specifically, children calling their parents by name, the concept of children moving out soon after they reach adulthood, and revealing clothing were sources of concern. In conservative Indian families, girls were (and still are) expected to wear modest clothing. American clothing staples like shorts, tank tops, and skirts didn't seem modest at all. In modern times, some amount of westernization is accepted alongside Indian culture.

The current generation expresses their thoughts on assimilation through stories. A Bollywood movie called *Pardes* took on the subject of the struggle of becoming American. The title translates to "foreign land." The movie follows an Indian woman arriving in the United States after her engagement to a wealthy nonresident Indian (NRI). Her Indian culture and her husband's completely westernized personality conflict repeatedly, resulting in a mixing of two incompatible cultures. The protagonist ends up marrying a man who has also embraced Western culture but retains his Indian values. The man is a symbol of the Indian American generation and proudly identifies as being both Indian and Western in an American homeland.

The release of comedian Hasan Minhaj's stand-up comedy film *Homecoming King* also told an immigrant narrative. A significant detail of his story was his marriage to his Hindu wife, Beena Patel. Minhaj, an Indian American Muslim, broke the tradition of marrying someone of the same religion. This was a notable milestone because Hindus and Muslims have clashed since the sixteenth century, and the fights were the cause of the 1947 Indian partition.

Comedian Hasan Minhaj has notable roles on *The Daily Show*, as well as *Homecoming King*, in which he focuses on his struggles and experiences as a child of Indian immigrants to America.

Another facet that contributes to the identity struggle is the attitude toward LGBTQ+ people. Gender and sex norms span international borders, and India is no exception. Homosexuality is still a taboo in several regions of India. For gay Indians living in the West, it is a relief to find much more support for the LGBTQ+ movement.

THREATS TO THE INDIAN AMERICAN DREAM

When the September 11, 2001, terrorist attacks in New York City, Washington, DC, and Pennsylvania killed 2,996 people and injured 6,000, a wave of backlash to the South Asian and Middle Eastern community followed. Ignorance caused nativist attackers in the United States to target turban-wearing men and profile those victims as terrorists. Because al-Qaeda, the organization behind the attacks, was a radical Islamist group, nativist attackers and less violent actors targeted Muslim Americans and subjected them to various forms of abuse.

While individual attacks against immigrants and American-born Indians became a disturbingly regular occurrence that lost traction in media representation, other incidents attempted to destroy whole communities. On August 5, 2012, lone shooter Wade Michael Page, a white supremacist, shot and killed six Sikh temple goers and injured three others before shooting himself in a mass killing spree at an Oak Creek, Wisconsin, Sikh temple.

The Wisconsin Sikh temple was not the last incident of such violence. In 2017, a white supremacist who yelled "You don't belong here!" to Indian engineer Srinivas Kuchibhotla shot and killed Kuchibhotla at a Kansas bar. Kuchibhotla was a successful tech worker. His death, as with every attack against members of the community, caused the vision of the American Dream to falter in the eyes of Indian immigrants.

Under President Donald Trump, the United States continues to face dramatic changes. Trump signed an executive

The death of Indian engineer Srinivas Kuchibhotla sparked shock and sorrow. His picture is seen at a peace demonstration in Washington on March 5, 2017.

order to review the H-1B visa program in July 2017. Now, the number of H-1B visas will likely decrease. Trump is likely to push policies that fulfill the promise of the slogan "Buy American and hire American," which was similar to the demands and work of the AEL of the 1900s.

PERSEVERANCE AND THE FIGHT FOR HOME

When Indian American Piyush "Bobby" Jindal became governor of Louisiana in 2007 and then Nimrata "Nikki" Haley became the governor of South Carolina in 2010, the message was clear: Indians were here to stay and represent their communities, both Indian and American. Entertainers like Aziz Ansari and Mindy Kaling continue to win hearts through laughter and positivity. Novelists like Jhumpa Lahiri weave colorful stories of the way that Indian culture lives and breathes in America. The 2016 development that allowed Indians to keep turbans and beards as US soldiers was another sign of a changing society. The collective narrative of Indians in the media and in local communities is one of strength and resilience.

The Indian community is also changing with its environment. Typically, the community does not tolerate cultural violations. In 1999, homosexuality and transgender identities were considered to be cultural violations because of residual expectations that the British Raj had imposed. That is why Parag Mehta was ashamed of his sexuality and struggled

South Carolina governor Nikki Haley and Louisiana governor Bobby Jindal sit together at a National Governors Association meeting at the White House on February 27, 2017.

with hiding his sexuality from his family. He even attempted suicide on two occasions.

Mehta came out to his family in 1999. The worst-case scenario was that they and his community would shun him, but his immediate family was accepting of his revelation. The Indian community where he lived, however, was not so accepting of his sexual identity. Still, Mehta and his family sought acceptance from their community in an attempt to change their values to be more welcoming. Mehta went on to work with Barack Obama in forging relationships with the LGBTQ+ community in the United States. He was the first liaison to the LGBTQ+ community at the White House and pushed for a new milestone in the Indian community: the growth of lesbian and gay acceptance.

Indians continue to be one of the fastest-growing ethnic groups in the United States, even if they aren't changing their cultural norms as quickly. Their contributions to American society are also increasing. Indian physicians are a significant presence across the country. Indian engineers and scientists are making discoveries in Silicon Valley and elsewhere. Indian educators have found their niche in American schools, and Indian political activists and local citizens have moved toward greater contributions in government.

According to the National Academies of Sciences, Engineering, and Medicine survey, one in four immigrants successfully integrates into US society. Immigration reports from 2015 indicated that 45 percent of 2.4 million Indian immigrants were naturalized. In the same year, nearly 3.5 million Indian Americans were living in the United States, as either immigrants or native-born citizens—numbers that far exceed the earlier, restricted presence of Indians in the United States. Today, the Indian diaspora thrives and stands tall despite the difficulties that surround them.

MYTHS AND FACTS

Myth
Indians marry only within their community.

Fact
Marrying within the ethnic community used to be a common societal expectation in earlier decades of Indian immigration to the United States. Indian immigrants and Americans alike expected the separation to remain intact. However, marriage outside one's group is and always has been possible. Now, it is more accepted but infrequent within the Indian community compared to other ethnic groups.

Myth
Indian immigrants come to the United States to replace native-born workers in several occupations.

Fact
Indians were once used as a cheaper source of labor and as laborers who would break strikes. However, modern-day labor law in the United States has means to prevent unequal pay. There are still advantages to preferring foreign laborers. Visas are often granted to individuals who seek jobs in sectors that have an insufficient supply of workers, like information technology. But hiring a skilled worker from another country doesn't mean that that person is taking a job from a native-born worker. Native-born workers initially

(continued on the next page)

(continued from the previous page)

weren't hired for the same jobs because they lacked the skills, training, or experience to be successful. Even in the absence of foreign laborers, unprepared native workers are not hired. Many immigrant entrepreneurs, like Indian American Bose Corporation founder Amar Bose, also continue to shape the American economy by creating jobs. Overall, immigrants increase the availability of jobs instead of reducing it.

Myth

Indians only seek to become doctors, lawyers, and engineers.

Fact

Parents in many cultures try to motivate or influence their children to aspire to prestigious careers like medicine, law, and engineering. Like those from many cultures, however, Indian people pursue careers across the spectrum of possibilities. Finance, where senior analysts are paid a median income of $81,000, is another common field that Indians pursue. Indian writers like early Indian immigrant Bharati Mukhereei and modern-day novelist and Pulitzer Prize winner Jhumpa Lahiri are examples of successful people who haven't pursued medicine, law, or engineering.

INDIAN AMERICANS

Population

According to 2016 estimates from the US Census Bureau, there are approximately 4.12 million Indian Americans living in the United States.

Places

States with large Indian immigrant communities are California, Illinois, New Jersey, New York, and Texas.

The largest Hindu temple is the Bochasanwasi Akshar Purushottam Swaminarayan Sanstha, which is located in Robbinsville, New Jersey. It is 42 feet (13 meters) high and 133 feet (40.5 meters) wide. Shastriji Maharaj, an Indian, established it on June 5, 1907.

Ethnicities and Religions

The majority of Indian Americans, 51 percent, identify as Hindus. Of Indian Americans, 18 percent identify as Christians, and 10 percent identify as Muslims. There is a small number of Sikhs, Jains, and observers of other religions.

The top five Indian languages spoken in the United States are Hindi, Gujarati, Punjabi, Tamil, and Telugu.

Punjabi Mexican American children, sometimes called Mexican Hindus, had fused names such as Yolanda Singh or Jose Akbar

Singh. They carried the last names of their Indian fathers and the first names chosen by their Spanish-speaking mothers.

Education

In 2013, 76 percent of Indian immigrants older than twenty-five were reported to have a bachelor's degree or higher.

Politics

Among Indian Americans, 65 percent identify as Democrats or lean toward the Democratic Party.

Food

Common foods of the Indian diet include roti, a circular flatbread, and sabzi, a spiced vegetable or meat dish. Indians and other ethnic groups across the world love naan, a puffier flatbread.

Notable People

Dr. Yellapragada Subbarow helped develop Methotrexate, a chemotherapy treatment that is still used.

Salman Khan started the Khan Academy, a free online education platform.

Padma Lakshmi is an author, model, and television show host.

Holidays

Diwali is a major Hindu holiday, also called the Festival of Lights. People celebrate it by lighting several lamps, candles, and fireworks, and by conducting prayers. It marks the victory of the Hindu Lord Rama in a battle against the demon Ravana. Vaisakhi is a day that Sikhs and Hindus celebrate. It marks the spring harvest and is also the New Year for the Sikh religion. One of the largest celebrations takes place in New York City. Thousands of Sikhs take part in a parade near Madison Square Park in Manhattan. The free community meal known as *langar* and the festivities are open to the public.

Muslims, including those who emigrated from India, celebrate a holiday called Eid al-Fitr. Eid al-Fitr is the day of religious celebration and festivities that takes place after a month of fasting called Ramadan. Prayers take place in mosques and outdoor locations.

Muslims celebrate a second holy celebration, Eid al-Adha. Eid al-Adha is also known as Great Eid, and it commemorates the willingness of Ibrahim (Abraham), an important figure in Abrahamic religions, to sacrifice his son. Activities include the slaughter of lambs as a form of religious devotion, donations to the poor, and family gatherings.

TIMELINE

1608 The British East India Company arrives at the port of Surat, Gujarat.

1858 The British Raj rises in India. It rapidly colonizes several Indian states using the financial leverage of the East India Trading Company.

1905 The Asiatic Exclusion League is created in the United States to oppose immigrant laborers, including Indians.

1907 The Bellingham riots in Washington cause the entire community of Indian immigrants to flee Bellingham. Police jail 410 Indians, supposedly for their safety. Six are hospitalized.

1912 The first Indian religious center, a Sikh gurdwara in Stockton, California, is established.

1913 The California Alien Land Law is passed to prevent people not eligible to become citizens from owning American land.

Punjabi Sikhs in the United States form the Ghadar Party, an organization that opposed the British Raj.

Akhay Kumar Mozumdar becomes the first Indian immigrant to be naturalized.

1914 World War I begins.

1917 Congress passes the Immigration Act of 1917, and Asians are banned from participating in US immigration.

1923 The ruling in *United States v. Bhagat Singh Thind* rescinds the citizenship of Thind, as well as other high-caste Hindus of Indian blood, and declares that they are not eligible for citizenship.

1924 President Calvin Coolidge signs the Immigration Act of 1924, which dictates that only 2 percent of the present number of a racial group be allowed to immigrate each year.

Indians launch the Quit India movement.

1939 World War II begins.

1946 President Harry Truman signs the Luce-Celler Act of 1946, allowing one hundred Indians and Filipinos each year to immigrate. They are also permitted to naturalize and own property.

1947 India gains its independence. The country is partitioned into India and Pakistan (then consisting of Pakistan and modern-day Bangladesh).

1953 Indian astrophysicist Subrahmanyan Chandrasekhar becomes a naturalized citizen.

1957 Dalip Singh Saund, the first Indian immigrant in US government, begins his first term as a representative in Congress for the Twenty-Ninth District of California.

1965 President Lyndon B. Johnson signs the Immigration Nationality Act of 1965 to abolish the quota system based on national origins so that one country's citizens are no longer preferred over another's.

1984 Sikhs are persecuted in a genocide in India for their religious affiliation with the assassinators of then prime minister Indira Gandhi. Many Sikhs flee to the United States, Canada, and the United Kingdom.

1987 Racist attacks by a gang called the Dotbusters plague New Jersey Indian residents.

1991 India extends more freedom to the private sector and enables accelerated growth of India's engineering district.

2001 Al-Qaeda orchestrates September 11 terrorist attacks.

2007 Piyush "Bobby" Jindal is elected governor of Louisiana.

2010 Nimrata "Nikki" Haley becomes the governor of South Carolina.

2012 Wade Michael Page shoots six people to death and injures three before killing himself in a mass shooting at a Sikh temple.

2016 The US Army allows Sikh soldiers to wear turbans and beards.

2017 A white supremacist named Adam Purinton shoots Indian engineer Srinivas Kuchibhotla to death in a Kansas bar.

President Trump signs an executive order to revise the H-1B visa program.

autonomy Control over the self, or a state of not being oppressed and being forced into making decisions against one's interest.

capitalist A person, group, or institution that supports private business ownership and allows the owner to set prices for its products, decide how much to make, and other decisions that involve conducting business. In a capitalist system, the government doesn't cause the business owner to act against his or her will.

credit The amount of money that one is obligated to pay back.

cultural appropriation Participating in an aspect of a culture other than one's own for the purposes of looking exotic or cool instead of as a way of observing the practices and beliefs of that culture. Considered an act of theft.

debt foreclosure Being forced to give up a piece of property in order to pay for a debt that one cannot pay back voluntarily.

diaspora A community of people who have been dispersed throughout different lands.

diminish To decrease.

emigration Permanently leaving one's home country to live somewhere else.

exogamy Marrying outside of one's tribe or group.

feudal system A system of rule in which a ruler is an owner of land who allows subjects to use some of that land in exchange for services or labor.

homogeneous Having the characteristic of uniformity or sameness.

immigration Coming into and settling in a new country.

naturalization The process of becoming a country's citizen.

quota A limit on a number of items or people.

revenue A company's income over a period of time.

sepoy Indian military recruits for the British army.

tolerance Accepting the existence of actions, behavior, or beliefs that one does not agree with or are different from one's own.

visa A legal certification on a passport that authorizes a person to enter, leave, or stay in a country.

westernization The process of making something European or American.

white supremacy The belief that white people are superior to people of other races and should be able to control nonwhite people. Or the belief that white people should receive priority over nonwhite people in institutions like education, health care, and protection under the law.

xenophobia Hatred or fear of people who are different in some way, such as being from a different ethnic group, race, or country.

zamindars Landlords who exploited the law to keep laborers in debt.

American Association of Physicians of Indian Origin
600 Enterprise Drive #108
Oak Brook, IL 60523
(630) 990-2277
Website: https://www.aapiusa.org
Facebook: @AmericanAssociationofPhysiciansofIndianOrigin
Twitter: @AAPIUSA
This association of Indian physicians works to provide the best health care to American communities. There are chapters in twenty states.

Association of Indians in America
26 Pleasant Lane
Oyster Bay, NY 11771
(516) 624-2460
Website: http://www.theaiany.org
Facebook: @theaiany
Founded in 1967, this is the oldest national Indian American organization. It supports the success and development of the Indian community in the United States.

Canada-India Centre for Excellence
Carleton University, 1401R-F
Richcraft Hall, 1125 Colonel By Drive
Ottawa, ON K1S 5B6
Canada
(613) 520-2600 x7873
Website: https://carleton.ca/india
This center leads research initiatives and professionally trains

students around Indo-Canada ties. Some projects include work on smart cities.

Desis Rising Up and Moving (DRUM)
72-18 Roosevelt Avenue
Jackson Heights, NY 11372
(718) 205-3036
Website: http://www.drumnyc.org
Facebook: @DesisRising
Twitter: @DesisRisingUp
Founded in 2000, DRUM works for the social and economic betterment of low-wage South Asian immigrants.

Indo-Canada Ottawa Business Chamber (ICOBC)
251 Laurier Avenue West, Suite 900
Ottawa, ON, K1P 5J6
(613) 696-4262
Website: http://www.icobc.org
Facebook: @ICOBC
The ICOBC organizes funding programs to improve Indo-Canada trade relations. It holds conferences and seminars for the sake of economic betterment.

National Queer Asian Pacific Islander Alliance
1322 18th Street NW
Washington, DC 20036
(917) 439-3158
Website: http://www.nqapia.org/wpp
Facebook: @NQAPIA

Twitter: @NQAPIA
This alliance helps to organize local groups that deal with issues concerning LGBTQ+ people in all Asian and Asian American communities.

South Asian Americans Leading Together
6930 Carroll Avenue, Suite 506
Takoma Park, MD 20912
(301) 270-1855
Website: http://saalt.org
Facebook: @talktosaalt
Twitter: @SAALTweets
This national civil rights organization works to provide legal support to South Asian Americans. Its mission is centered on attaining social justice for residents.

FOR FURTHER READING

Alyan, Hala. *Hijra: Poems*. Carbondale, IL: Crab Orchard Review & Southern Illinois University Press, 2016.

Bhaneja, Balwant. *Troubled Pilgrimage: Passage to Pakistan*. Toronto, ON: TSAR, 2013.

Das, Ashidhara. *Desi Dreams: Indian Immigrant Women Build Lives Across Two Worlds*. Delhi, India: Primus Books, 2012.

Ejaz, Khadija. *My Friend is Hindu*. Kennett Square, PA: Purple Toad Publishing, 2015.

Faelli, Rita. *Islam*. New York, NY: AV^2 by Weigl, 2016.

Katoch, Dhruv C., Quazi Sajjad Ali Zahir, and Indian War Veterans Association. *Liberation: Bangladesh–1971*. New Delhi, India: Bloomsbury Publishing India Pvt. Ltd., 2015.

Rehman, Sabeeha. *Threading My Prayer Rug: One Woman's Journey from Pakistani Muslim to American Muslim*. New York, NY: Arcade Publishing, 2016.

Tharoor, Sashi. *India: From Midnight to the Millennium and Beyond.* New York, NY: Aracade Publishing, 2012.

Tripathi, Laxmi Narayan, R. Raj Rao, and P. G. Joshi. *Me Hijra, Me Laxmi*. New Delhi, India: Oxford University Press, 2015.

White-Spunner, Barney. *Partition: The Story of Indian Independence and the Creation of Pakistan in 1947*. New York, NY: Simon & Schuster, 2017.

BIBLIOGRAPHY

Asiatic Exclusion League. Proceedings of the A.E.L. July 16, 1911. Reproduced at http://pluralism.org/document/the-asiatic-exclusion-league.

Basi, Moni. "After Attacks, Indian Immigrants Reconsider the American Dream." CNN, March 11, 2017. http://www.cnn.com/2017/03/10/us/indian-immigrants-american-dream/index.html.

Batalova, Jeanne, and Jie Zong. "Indian Immigrants in the United States." Migration Policy, August 31, 2017. http://www.migrationpolicy.org/article/indian-immigrants-united-states.

Becker, Elizabeth. "Military Has Severe Doctor Shortage" *Washington Post*, June 7, 1977. https://www.washingtonpost.com/archive/politics/1977/06/07/military-has-severe-doctor-shortage/eaaeb462-4252-486a-8fa8-c4f5c9cf8ab4/?utm_term=.e45784f4f6c8

Bhatia, Sunil. *American Karma*. New York, NY: New York University Press, 2007.

Bhattaccharyya, Anirudh. "Ontario Passes Motion Calling 1984 Riots Genocide, India Says Move Misguided." *Hindustan Times*, April 8, 2017. http://www.hindustantimes.com/world-news/ontario-passes-motion-describing-1984-anti-sikh-riots-as-genocide/story-1YPs2tiMkvtW2Tp7UDyydK.html.

Biswas, Bidisha, and Vijaya Ramya. *Indian Immigrant Women and Work: The American Experience*. Abingdon, UK: Routledge, 2016.

Buchanan, Daniel Houston. *The Development of Capitalistic Enterprise in India*. Abingdon, UK: Routledge, 1966.

Chakravorty, Sanjoy, Devesh Kapur, and Nirvikar Singh. *The Other One Percent: Indians in America*. New York, NY: Oxford University Press, 2017.

Chazen Global Insights. "A Singular Population: Indian Immigrants in America." Columbia University, February 22, 2017. https://www8.gsb.columbia.edu/articles/chazen-global-insights/singular-population-indian-immigrants-america.

Howard, David. "Yesterday's Evangelist from India." The Universal Message. Retrieved September 25, 2017. http://www.mozumdar.org/yesterdaysevangelist.html.

Kang, Jasbir Singh. "Punjabi Migration to United States: A Story of Great Tenacity." Sikh Foundation. Retrieved September 25, 2017. http://www.sikhfoundation.org/PunjabiMigration_JSKang.html.

Marriot, Michael. "In Jersey City, Indians Protest Violence." *New York Times*, October 12, 1987. http://www.nytimes.com/1987/10/12/nyregion/in-jersey-city-indians-protest-violence.html.

Pinsky, Mark. "The Mexican-Hindu Connection: In a Search for Their Roots, Descendants Discover a Moving Tale of Loneliness and Racism." *Los Angeles Times*, December 21, 1987. http://articles.latimes.com/1987-12-21/news/vw-20399_1_mexican-women.

Purkayastha, Bandana. *Negotiating Ethnicity: Second-Generation South Asians Traverse a Transnational World.* Piscataway, NJ: Rutgers University Press, 2003.

Pusey, Grace. "Today in History: Luce-Celler Act Signed in 1946." SAADA, July 2, 2014. https://www.saada.org/news/20140702-3609.

Saund, Dalip Singh. *Congressman from India*. New York, NY: E. P. Dutton and Company, 1960.

Smith, Marian, and Peter Hammerschmidt. *Indian Immigration* (The Changing Face of North America: Immigration Since 1965). Broomall, PA: Mason Crest Publishing, 2004.

Tamkin, Emily. "Interview: Indian Immigration in the Time of Trump." *Foreign Policy*, March 8, 2017. http://foreignpolicy.com/2017/03/08/interview-indian-immigration-in-the-time-of-trump.

WITW staff. "Wives of Silicon Valley's Immigrant Engineers Speak of Loneliness and Frustration." Women in the World, May 20, 2016. http://nytlive.nytimes.com/womenintheworld/2016/05/20/wives-of-silicon-valleys-immigrant-engineers-speak-of-loneliness-and-frustration.

INDEX

ABOUT THE AUTHOR

Paramjot Kaur received her bachelor of arts in economics from New York University in 2018. Kaur's work has been published overseas with humanitarian organizations and the United Nations Association of America. As an avid activist for social betterment and equality, she participates in United Nations initiatives and is a proud supporter of diverse communities. Her focus is on the economic empowerment of citizens in developing countries and creating policies for empowering women. This book has a personal connection for her because she and her family emigrated from India to America.

PHOTO CREDITS

Cover, p. 3 Jihan Abdalla/Blend Images/Getty Images; pp. 6–7 © British Library Board. All Rights Reserved/Bridgeman Images; p. 11 Library of Congress Geography and Map Division; p. 15 Courtesy of The Universal Message (www.mozumdar.org); p. 17 Holt-Atherton Special Collections, University of the Pacific Library; p. 21 Courtesy of the Department of Special Collections, Stanford University Libraries; p. 26 melanzane1013/Flickr/Emma Lazarus plaque/CC BY-SA 2.0; p. 28 ullstein bild/Getty Images; p. 32 Keystone-France/Gamma-Keystone/Getty Images; p. 35 J. R. Eyerman/The LIFE Picture Collection/Getty Images; p. 36 Robert Knudsen. White House Photographs. John F. Kennedy Presidential Library and Museum, Boston; p. 38 LBJ Library photo by Yoichi Okamoto; p. 42 © AP Images; p. 44 Noah Seelam/AFP /Getty Images; p. 48 STF/AFP/Getty Images; p. 52 Chandan Khanna/AFP /Getty Images; p. 55 James Devaney/Getty Images; p. 57 Jason Redmond /AFP/Getty Images; p. 59 Chip Somodevilla/Getty Images; interior pages designs (portrait collage) Ollyy/Shutterstock.com, (USA stamp) ducu59us /Shutterstock.com, (fingerprint) Rigamondis/Shutterstock.com, (brochure) Konstanin L/Shutterstock.com, (visa) Sergiy Palamarchuk/Shutterstock.com.

Design: Nelson Sá; Layout: Nicole Russo-Duca; Photo Researcher: Nicole DiMella